WHEN WINTER COMES

Copyright © 1989 American Teacher Publications

Published by Raintree Publishers Limited Partnership

Library of Congress number: 89-3595

Library of Congress Cataloging in Publication Data.

Neuman, Pearl.
  When winter comes / Pearl Neuman; illustrated by Richard Roe.

  (Real readers)
  Summary: Explains how the woodchuck, black bear, red fox, and Canada goose cope with winter in the northern parts of North America.
  [1. Mammals—North America—Wintering—Juvenile literature. 2.   Canada goose—North America—Wintering—Juvenile literature. [1. Animals—Wintering. 2. Winter.]
I. Roe, Richard, 1959-   ill. II. Title. III. Series.
  QL715.N45 1989 599′.054′3097—dc19   89-3595
ISBN 0-8172-3519-1

    2 3 4 5 6 7 8 9 0   93 92 91 90 89

REAL READERS

WHEN WINTER COMES

by Pearl Neuman
illustrated by Richard Roe

Raintree Publishers
Milwaukee

In some places, when **winter** comes, it gets very cold. Snow falls on the ground.

People who live where the winters are cold can put on warm coats. They can stay warm in houses, too. They can still get food.

But how do animals in the woods stay warm? How do they get food? What do animals do when winter comes?

Here is a woodchuck with grass in its mouth. It uses the grass to make a nest under the ground.

When it has made the nest, the woodchuck eats lots of the grass and green leaves. By the time winter comes, the woodchuck is fat.

On the very first cold day, the woodchuck goes into its nest. It takes some grass and uses it to plug up the hole to the outside.

Then the woodchuck closes its eyes, curls up in a ball, and goes to sleep.

The woodchuck sleeps all winter long. It sleeps all day and all night. It doesn't need to go out or get up to eat. It lives on its fat all winter long.

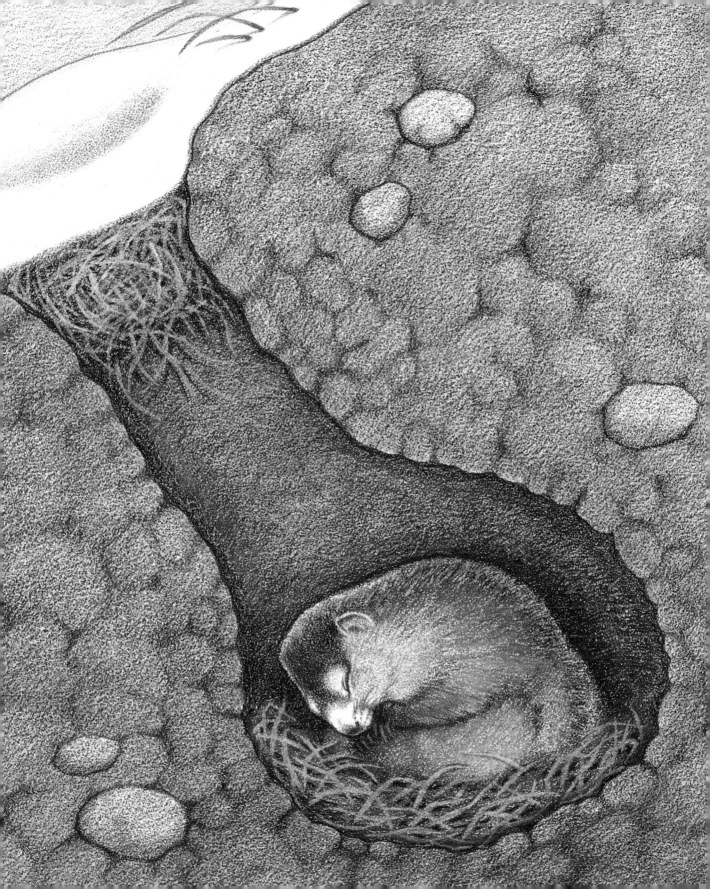

Here is a black bear out for a walk. Before the first snow, it must find somewhere to sleep. The black bear looks for a safe place in a cave or a log. It looks for a good spot under the trees.

The black bear finds a place to sleep. Now it is set for the winter. It has a home where it can spend the cold days. The black bear sleeps on a grass bed. It sleeps in the day, and it sleeps at night, too.

But the black bear does not sleep as long as the woodchuck does. The woodchuck sleeps all winter. The black bear wakes up from time to time. On some days, the black bear leaves its cave and goes looking for plants or animals to eat.

Here is a red fox at work before winter. It digs a deep hole to hide some of its food. It packs away food for the winter, when it is hard to find food.

On winter days that are warm, the red fox will go out to look for fresh food. On a walk in the woods, the fox sees a mouse. The red fox dives down in the snow to try and grab the mouse. The mouse can be food for the red fox.

Here are some birds that fly **south** for the winter. The birds are called Canada geese. When winter comes, they fly south from Canada to Florida or California.

Why do Canada geese fly south? In winter, it is hard for the geese to find food. It is cold and the plants they like to eat stop growing. It is warm in the south. There are plants there for the geese to eat. They fly south to find food.

We know this because people in Canada sometimes put out food for the geese. When they do, the geese stay in Canada for the winter.

In the **summer**, the geese fly back to the **north**. In the summer it is hard for the geese to find food and water in the south. It is very dry there. The geese fly north to Canada to find food.

What do animals do in the winter? Some sleep like the woodchuck. Some sleep and wake like the bear. Some pack away food like the red fox does. When there's no food, some leave home like the Canada geese.

Each animal does what it needs to to stay warm and get food when winter comes.

Sharing the Joy of Reading

Beginning readers enjoy reading books on their own. Reading a book is a worthwhile activity in and of itself for a young reader. However, a child's reading can be even more rewarding if it is shared. This sharing can enhance your child's appreciation—both of the book and of his or her own abilities.

Now that your child has read **When Winter Comes**, you can help extend your child's reading experience by encouraging him or her to:

- Retell the story or key concepts presented in this story in his or her own words. The retelling can be oral or written.

- Create a picture of a favorite character, event, or concept from this book.

- Express his or her own ideas and feelings about the subject of this book and other things he or she might want to know about this subject.

Here is a special activity that you and your child can do together to further extend the appreciation of this book: You and your child can do some observations and/or research during the winter months. If you live in a place where winters are cold, you and your child could watch what kinds of birds stay around for the winter months. If you live in a warm climate, you may have new birds in your area for the winter months. You may want to set up a bird feeding station to attract the birds or feed birds in a park near your home.